ANIMALS

QUIZ BOOK
FOR SHARP MINDS

A wonderful book for the whole Family!

Copyright © 2023 by Sharp Minds Learning

ALL RIGHTS RESERVED

No part of this book may be reproduced, stored in a retrieval system, or transmitted in any form or by any means, electronic, mechanical, photocopying, recording, scanning, or otherwise, without the prior written permission of the publisher.

Content

Introduction 4
Quiz # 1 - Mammals 5
Quiz # 2 - Wildlife 9
Quiz # 3 - Birds 13
Quiz # 4 - Marine Life 17
Quiz # 5 - Baby Animals 21
Quiz # 6 - Pet Animals 25
Quiz # 7 - National Animals 29
Quiz # 8 - Reptiles & Amphibians 33
Quiz # 9 - Animals Extreme 37
Quiz # 10 - Groups of Animals 41
Quiz # 11 - Animals Anatomy 45
Quiz # 12 - Desert Dwellers 49
Quiz # 13 - Animals Feeding Styles 53
Quiz # 14 - Deadliest Animals 57
Quiz # 15 - All about Dogs 61
Quiz # 16 - All about Cats 65
Quiz # 17 - Endangered Species 69
Quiz # 18 - Prehistoric Creatures 73
Quiz # 19 - Animals Senses 77
Quiz # 20 - Animals Behavior & Communication 81
Answers 86

INTRODUCTION

Welcome to "Animals Quiz Book for Sharp Minds"! Are you ready to embark on a thrilling exploration of the fascinating world of animals? This book delves into the captivating realm of Earth's diverse creatures, their habitats, behaviors, and the incredible variety of life that inhabits our planet.

"Animals Quiz Book for Sharp Minds" has been meticulously curated to challenge your animal knowledge, ignite your curiosity, and take you on an enthralling journey through the animal kingdom. Whether you're a wildlife enthusiast, an aspiring zoologist, or someone who finds joy in learning about the creatures we share our world with, this book is tailor-made to entertain and educate.

This book aims to enrich your understanding of the animal kingdom and provide an avenue for delightful and thought-provoking quizzes and challenges. Whether you're flipping through these pages solo, engaging in friendly competition with friends and family, or utilizing this book as an invaluable resource for educators and students, "Animals Quiz Book for Sharp Minds" promises to kindle your passion for animals and expand your horizons.

So, let's embark on this thrilling adventure together and uncover the wonders of the animal world.

Are you ready to put your animal knowledge to the test?

Quiz # 1

Mammals

Q#1

Which mammal is known for its ability to fly?

A) Puma
B) Koala
C) Armadillo
D) Bat

Q#2

Which mammal is native to Australia and known for carrying its young in a pouch?

A) Kangaroo
B) Panda
C) Cheetah
D) Hippopotamus

Q#3

What is the fastest land mammal?

A) Bear
B) Cheetah
C) Bison
D) Chimpanzee

Answers on Page # 86

Quiz # 1 - Mammals

Q#4

Which mammal is known as the "King of the Jungle"?

A) Tiger
B) Leopard
C) Lion
D) Hyena

Q#5

What mammal is native to the Arctic and known for its thick fur and white coloration?

A) Seal
B) Arctic Fox
C) Polar Bear
D) Walrus

Q#6

Which mammal is known for its long, prehensile tail and is native to South America?

A) Zebra
B) Giraffe
C) Rhinoceros
D) Sloth

Q#7

What is the national mammal of the United States?

A) Bison
B) Raccoon
C) Gray Wolf
D) Bald Eagle

Answers on Page # 86

Quiz # 1 - Mammals

Q#8
Which mammal is famous for its black and white markings and is native to China?

A) Tiger
B) Koala
C) Giant Panda
D) Meerkat

Q#9
What is the largest species of whale?

A) Bottlenose Dolphin
B) Humpback Whale
C) Narwhal
D) Blue Whale

Q#10
Which mammal is known for its hibernation and is often associated with honey?

A) Grizzly Bear
B) Moose
C) Honey Badger
D) Polar Bear

Q#11
Which mammal is known for its ability to regenerate lost body parts?

A) Hedgehog
B) Axolotl
C) Mole
D) Lemur

Answers on Page # 86

Quiz # 1 - Mammals

Q#12
Which mammal is famous for its black and white stripes?

A) Chimpanzee
B) Gorilla
C) Zebra
D) Lemur

Q#13
Which mammal is known for laying eggs instead of giving birth to live young?

A) Manatee
B) Hedgehog
C) Dolphin
D) Platypus

Q#14
What animal has the longest pregnancy?

A) Lemur
B) Elephant
C) Wolverine
D) Ocelot

Q#15
Which mammal is known for its ability to roll into a ball as a defense mechanism?

A) Kangaroo
B) Hedgehog
C) Lemur
D) Armadillo

Answers on Page # 86

Quiz # 2

Wildlife

Q#1

What is the largest species of big cat found in South America jungles?

A) Puma
B) Bengal Tiger
C) Jaguar
D) Leopard

Q#2

Which large herbivorous mammal is native to Africa and known for its long trunk?

A) Elephant
B) Rhinoceros
C) Giraffe
D) Hippopotamus

Q#3

What is the world's smallest species of bear?

A) Grizzly Bear
B) Polar Bear
C) Panda Bear
D) Sun Bear

Answers on Page # 86

Quiz # 2 - Wildlife

Q#4

Which animal is famous for its long, spiral horns?

A) Antelope
B) Ibex
C) Giraffe
D) Bear

Q#5

Which jungle animal is known for its ability to swing through trees using its prehensile tail?

A) Kangaroo
B) Squirrel
C) Koala
D) Spider Monkey

Q#6

Which small, nocturnal primate is native to Madagascar?

A) Tarsier
B) Lemur
C) Bushbaby
D) Marmoset

Q#7

What is the world's largest species of antelope?

A) Impala
B) Springbok
C) Gazelle
D) Eland

Answers on Page # 86

Quiz # 2 - Wildlife

Q#8
Which marsupial is native to Australia and known for its leaping ability?

A) Koala
B) Wombat
C) Kangaroo
D) Tasmanian Devil

Q#9
Which large, slow-moving reptile is primarily found in the rivers and swamps of the southeastern United States?

A) Anaconda
B) Alligator
C) Python
D) Boa Constrictor

Q#10
What is the national bird of the United States, known for its distinctive white head and tail feathers?

A) Bald Eagle
B) American Robin
C) Peregrine Falcon
D) Northern Cardinal

Q#11
What is the term for the leader of a wolf pack?

A) Beta
B) Alpha
C) Omega
D) Zeta

Answers on Page # 86

Quiz # 2 - Wildlife

Q#12
What is the largest species of rhinoceros?

A) White Rhinoceros
B) Black Rhinoceros
C) Indian Rhinoceros
D) Javan Rhinoceros

Q#13
Which large, flightless bird is native to Africa and known for its strong legs and long neck?

A) Ostrich
B) Emu
C) Cassowary
D) Rhea

Q#14
What is the largest species of big cat found in Asia's jungles?

A) Puma
B) Bengal Tiger
C) Jaguar
D) Leopard

Q#15
Which big cat is known for its distinctive black mane?

A) Cheetah
B) Lion
C) Leopard
D) Jaguar

Answers on Page # 86

Quiz # 3

Birds

Q#1

Which bird is known for its colorful plumage and is often associated with the Amazon rainforest?

A) Toucan
B) Pigeon
C) Sparrow
D) Owl

Q#2

Which bird species is known for its habit of diving into water to catch fish with its sharp claws?

A) Eagle
B) Owl
C) Osprey
D) Vulture

Q#3

What is the smallest bird in the world?

A) Sparrow
B) Bee Hummingbird
C) Finch
D) Eagle

Answers on Page # 86

Quiz # 3 - Birds

Q#4
Which bird is known for its fast, aerial hunting and distinctive "screech"?

A) Owl
B) Hawk
C) Eagle
D) Falcon

Q#5
What do penguins use to propel themselves in the water?

A) Wings
B) Flippers
C) Fins
D) Tails

Q#6
Which bird is famous for its long, curved bill and is often seen wading in water to catch fish?

A) Stork
B) Crane
C) Heron
D) Pelican

Q#7
Which bird lays the largest egg relative to its size?

A) Eagle
B) Ostrich
C) Kiwi
D) Dove

Answers on Page # 86

Quiz # 3 - Birds

Q#8
What is the world's fastest flying bird?

A) Hawk
B) Sparrowhawk
C) Peregrine Falcon
D) Ostrich

Q#9
Which bird is known for its unique, nocturnal hooting calls?

A) Pigeon
B) Sparrow
C) Eagle Owl
D) Blue Jay

Q#10
What is the name for the female counterpart of a peacock?

A) Peacockess
B) Peahen
C) Poulard
D) Pheasant

Q#11
What is a group of owls called?

A) Flock
B) Herd
C) Parliament
D) Pod

Answers on Page # 86

Quiz # 3 - Birds

Q#12

What is the main diet of a flamingo that gives it its pink coloration?

A) Plankton
B) Insects
C) Fish
D) Red Berries

Q#13

Which bird is commonly regarded as a symbol of peace?

A) Sparrow
B) Eagle
C) Vulture
D) Dove

Q#14

What is the national bird of Canada, often seen in the country's wilderness?

A) Bald Eagle
B) Dove
C) Snowy Owl
D) Gray Jay

Q#15

What is the largest species of pigeon in the world?

A) Nicobar pigeon
B) Passenger pigeon
C) Victoria crowned pigeon
D) Rock pigeon

Answers on Page # 86

Quiz # 4

Marine Life

Q#1

What is the largest species of shark in the world?

A) Hammerhead Shark
B) Great White Shark
C) Whale Shark
D) Tiger Shark

Q#2

What is the term for a group of dolphins swimming together?

A) Flock
B) Herd
C) Pod
D) School

Q#3

Which marine mammal is known for its long tusks and is often associated with the Arctic?

A) Sea Lion
B) Seal
C) Beluga Whale
D) Narwhal

Answers on Page # 86

Quiz # 4 - Marine Life

Q#4
What is the largest species of ray, known for its flattened body and long tail?

A) Stingray
B) Manta Ray
C) Electric Ray
D) Eagle Ray

Q#5
Which tiny marine organism is responsible for producing most of Earth's oxygen?

A) Seaweed
B) Coral
C) Plankton
D) Sponge

Q#6
Which marine animal is known for its ability to change color and texture to blend in with its surroundings?

A) Seahorse
B) Cuttlefish
C) Clownfish
D) Sea Slug

Q#7
What is the world's smallest species of whale?

A) Humpback Whale
B) Dwarf Sperm Whale
C) Minke Whale
D) Fin Whale

Answers on Page # 86

Quiz # 4 - Marine Life

Q#8
Which marine animal is known for its ability to regrow lost limbs?

A) Starfish
B) Sea Anemone
C) Sea Urchin
D) Sea Cucumber

Q#9
Which marine animal has a transparent body?

A) Jellyfish
B) Sea Horse
C) Glass Eel
D) Ghost Crab

Q#10
Which marine animal is known for its bioluminescent display?

A) Sea Turtle
B) Octopus
C) Jellyfish
D) Firefly Squid

Q#11
What is the process by which marine plants and algae convert sunlight into energy?

A) Fermentation
B) Respiration
C) Digestion
D) Photosynthesis

Answers on Page # 86

Quiz # 4 - Marine Life

Q#12
What is the term for the underwater mountains and valleys found on the ocean floor?

A) Canyons
B) Trenches
C) Abyssal Plains
D) Seamounts

Q#13
What is the name of the colorful, flattened marine animal that often attaches itself to coral reefs?

A) Starfish
B) Sea Anemone
C) Jellyfish
D) Sea Urchin

Q#14
Which marine animal is commonly known as sea cow?

A) Manatee
B) Hippopotamus
C) Dolphin
D) Platypus

Q#15
What is the largest species of squid, known for its enormous eyes?

A) Humboldt Squid
B) Giant Squid
C) Cuttlefish
D) Octopus

Answers on Page # 86

Quiz # 5

Baby Animals

Q#1
What is a baby dog called?

A) Calf
B) Foal
C) Cub
D) Puppy

Q#2
What is a baby cat called?

A) Kitten
B) Pup
C) Chick
D) Calf

Q#3
What is a baby horse called?

A) Calf
B) Foal
C) Kid
D) Cub

Answers on Page # 86

Quiz # 5 - Baby Animals

Q#4
What is a baby lion called?

A) Cub
B) Fawn
C) Chick
D) Calf

Q#5
What is a baby deer called?

A) Kid
B) Fawn
C) Pup
D) Calf

Q#6
What is a baby cow called?

A) Cub
B) Chick
C) Foal
D) Calf

Q#7
What is a baby kangaroo called?

A) Chick
B) Foal
C) Pup
D) Joey

Answers on Page # 86

Quiz # 5 - Baby Animals

Q#8
What is a baby goat called?

A) Kid
B) Foal
C) Fawn
D) Calf

Q#9
What is a baby pig called?

A) Calf
B) Chick
C) Piglet
D) Foal

Q#10
What is a baby rabbit called?

A) Pup
B) Cub
C) Fawn
D) Kit

Q#11
What is a baby duck called?

A) Duckling
B) Calf
C) Joey
D) Pup

Answers on Page # 86

Quiz # 5 - Baby Animals

Q#12
What is a baby seal called?

A) Calf
B) Cub
C) Pup
D) Foal

Q#13
What is a baby elephant called?

A) Foal
B) Cub
C) Calf
D) Fawn

Q#14
What is a baby frog called?

A) Cub
B) Tadpole
C) Calf
D) Kid

Q#15
What is a baby turtle called?

A) Hatchling
B) Pup
C) Joey
D) Piglet

Answers on Page # 86

Quiz # 6

Pet Animals

Q#1
Which animal is often referred to as "man's best friend" ?

A) Cat
B) Parrot
C) Hamster
D) Dog

Q#2
Which bird species is known for its ability to mimic human speech and is a popular pet in many households?

A) Parrot
B) Canary
C) Finch
D) Budgerigar

Q#3
What is the most common type of pet fish kept in home aquariums?

A) Goldfish
B) Guppy
C) Betta Fish
D) Angelfish

Answers on Page # 86

Quiz # 6 - Pet Animals

Q#4

Which domesticated animal is raised for its wool, meat, and milk ?

A) Horse
B) Cow
C) Sheep
D) Dog

Q#5

What is the most popular pet in the US?

A) Dogs
B) Cats
C) Fish
D) Hamsters

Q#6

What is the average lifespan of a goldfish?

A) 5-10 years
B) 10-15 years
C) 15-20 years
D) 20-25 years

Q#7

What is the scientific name for the domestic cat?

A) Panthera leo
B) Felis catus
C) Canis lupus
D) Ursus arctos

Answers on Page # 86

Quiz # 6 - Pet Animals

Q#8
What is a group of cats called?

A) Herd
B) Flock
C) Clowder
D) Pod

Q#9
What is a male cat called?

A) Sire
B) Tom
C) Bull
D) Boar

Q#10
Which pet rabbit breed is known for its distinctive lop ears that hang down on either side of its head?

A) Flemish Giant
B) Rex
C) Holland Lop
D) Angora

Q#11
Which dog breed is known for its wrinkled skin?

A) Poodle
B) Dalmatian
C) Shar-Pei
D) Beagle

Answers on Page # 86

Quiz # 6 - Pet Animals

Q#12
What is a female horse called?

A) Colt
B) Stallion
C) Foal
D) Mare

Q#13
Which breed of cat is known for its lack of a tail?

A) Siamese
B) Bengal
C) Manx
D) Ragdoll

Q#14
Which pet is often associated with a "wheel" for exercise?

A) Ferret
B) Chinchilla
C) Guinea Pig
D) Hamster

Q#15
Which pet is known for its ability to change color to match its surroundings?

A) Chameleon
B) Iguana
C) Tortoise
D) Snake

Answers on Page # 86

Quiz # 7

National Animals

Q#1

Which country's national animal is the bald eagle?

A) United States
B) Canada
C) Australia
D) Brazil

Q#2

Which animal is the national symbol of South Africa?

A) Lion
B) Springbok
C) Elephant
D) Cheetah

Q#3

What is the national animal of Russia?

A) Brown Bear
B) Siberian Tiger
C) Snow Leopard
D) Wolf

Answers on Page # 87

Quiz # 7 - National Animals

Q#4
Which creature represents Pakistan as its national animal?

A) Horse
B) Snow Leopard
C) Markhor
D) Black Bear

Q#5
Which country's national animal is the giant panda?

A) Russia
B) India
C) Japan
D) China

Q#6
What is the national animal of Thailand?

A) Elephant
B) Tiger
C) Giant Panda
D) Siamese Cat

Q#7
What is the national animal of Argentina?

A) Llama
B) Rufous Hornero
C) Andean Condor
D) Tiger

Answers on Page # 87

Quiz # 7 - National Animals

Q#8
What is the national animal of Greece?

A) Dove
B) Dolphin
C) Eagle
D) Tiger

Q#9
Which animal is the national symbol of Brazil?

A) Jaguar
B) Toucan
C) Capybara
D) Macaw

Q#10
What is the national animal of the United Kingdom?

A) Bulldog
B) Hedgehog
C) Robin
D) Lion

Q#11
What is the national animal of New Zealand?

A) Kangaroo
B) Tuatara
C) Kiwi
D) Kakapo

Answers on Page # 87

Quiz # 7 - National Animals

Q#12

Which animal is the national symbol of Sweden?

A) Lynx
B) Moose
C) Elk
D) Horse

Q#13

What is the national bird of India?

A) Crow
B) Sparrow
C) Peacock
D) Pigeon

Q#14

What is the national animal of Nepal?

A) Snow Leopard
B) Goat
C) Red Panda
D) Cow

Q#15

What is the national animal of Canada?

A) Beaver
B) Moose
C) Polar Bear
D) Grizzly Bear

Answers on Page # 87

Quiz # 8

Reptiles & Amphibians

Q#1
What is the heaviest snake species in the world?

A) Python
B) Anaconda
C) Rattlesnake
D) King Cobra

Q#2
What is the largest species of turtle in the world?

A) Leatherback Turtle
B) Loggerhead Turtle
C) Green Sea Turtle
D) Box Turtle

Q#3
What is the largest species of frog in the world?

A) Bullfrog
B) Poison Dart Frog
C) Goliath Frog
D) Tree Frog

Answers on Page # 87

Quiz # 8 - Reptiles & Amphibians

Q#4

What is the term for the tough, scaly skin that covers a reptile's body?

A) Fur
B) Feathers
C) Scales
D) Furcula

Q#5

Which reptile is known for its long, sticky tongue used to catch insects?

A) Lizard
B) Alligator
C) Komodo Dragon
D) Chameleon

Q#6

What is the largest species of crocodile in the world?

A) American Crocodile
B) Nile Crocodile
C) Saltwater Crocodile
D) Spectacled Caiman

Q#7

Which snake is known for its distinctive rattling sound as a warning signal?

A) Rattlesnake
B) Anaconda
C) Python
D) King Cobra

Answers on Page # 87

Quiz # 8 - Reptiles & Amphibians

Q#8

What are the heat-sensing pits on the heads of vipers and pythons called?

A) Heat Sacs
B) Venom Ducts
C) Pit Organs
D) Thermal Senses

Q#9

Which reptile has a venomous bite that can deliver a deadly neurotoxin?

A) Iguana
B) Crocodile
C) Komodo Dragon
D) Cobra

Q#10

Which reptile is often called the "living fossil" because of its ancient lineage and is found in China?

A) Tuatara
B) Komodo Dragon
C) Iguana
D) Gharial

Q#11

What is the term for the process by which some reptiles, like lizards, can voluntarily shed and regrow their tails?

A) Tail Regeneration
B) Tail Amputation
C) Autotomy
D) Tail Fission

Answers on Page # 87

Quiz # 8 - Reptiles & Amphibians

Q#12

What is the term for the specialized pads on the feet of many amphibians that allow them to climb vertical surfaces?

A) Toe Pads
B) Sticky Pads
C) Suction Discs
D) Adhesive Plates

Q#13

Which lizard, known for its ability to run on water, is often called the "Jesus Christ lizard"?

A) Horned Lizard
B) Basilisk Lizard
C) Anole
D) Gila Monster

Q#14

What amphibian croaks loudly at night?

A) Salamander
B) Gecko
C) Newt
D) Frog

Q#15

What is the term for the protective, transparent scale covering a snake's eye?

A) Spectacle
B) Visor
C) Ocular Shield
D) Sclerotic Scale

Answers on Page # 87

Quiz # 9

Animals Extreme

Q#1

Which of the following is the world's fastest land animal?

A) Cheetah
B) Pronghorn
C) Lion
D) Greyhound

Q#2

Which snake holds the record for the longest venomous snake?

A) Inland Taipan
B) Black Mamba
C) Reticulated Python
D) King Cobra

Q#3

What is the largest species of sea turtle?

A) Loggerhead Sea Turtle
B) Green Sea Turtle
C) Leatherback Sea Turtle
D) Hawksbill Sea Turtle

Answers on Page # 87

Quiz # 9 - Animals Extreme

Q#4

What is the smallest breed of horse in the world?

A) Falabella
B) Miniature Horse
C) Shetland Pony
D) Welsh Pony

Q#5

Which animal has the longest tongue relative to its body size?

A) Chameleon
B) Giraffe
C) Elephant
D) Blue Whale

Q#6

What is the largest species of kangaroo?

A) Wallaroo
B) Eastern Grey Kangaroo
C) Western Grey Kangaroo
D) Red Kangaroo

Q#7

What is the world's smallest species of dolphin?

A) Orca
B) Bottlenose Dolphin
C) Hector's Dolphin
D) Dusky Dolphin

Answers on Page # 87

Quiz # 9 - Animals Extreme

Q#8
What is the largest known species of horse?

A) Shire Horse
B) Mustang
C) Arabian Horse
D) Breton Horse

Q#9
What is the world's smallest species of owl?

A) Great Horned Owl
B) Barn Owl
C) Snowy Owl
D) Elf Owl

Q#10
Which animal sleeps for the most hours per day?

A) Sloth
B) Koala
C) Lion
D) Bat

Q#11
Which bird can mimic the widest range of sounds and calls?

A) Parrot
B) Mockingbird
C) Lyrebird
D) Starling

Answers on Page # 87

Quiz # 9 - Animals Extreme

Q#12

Which animal has the fastest heart rate, beating up to 1,000 times per minute?

A) Hummingbird
B) Cheetah
C) Rabbit
D) Pronghorn

Q#13

What is the largest species of rodent?

A) Brown Rat
B) Beaver
C) Squirrel
D) Capybara

Q#14

What is the smallest species of fox?

A) Arctic Fox
B) Fennec Fox
C) Red Fox
D) Grey Fox

Q#15

Which of these animals has the most teeth?

A) Snail
B) Shark
C) Tiger
D) Crocodile

Answers on Page # 87

Quiz # 10

Groups of Animals

Q#1
What is a group of lions called?

A) Herd
B) Pod
C) Pride
D) Flock

Q#2
What is a group of fish called?

A) School
B) Troop
C) Pack
D) Herd

Q#3
What is a group of wolves called?

A) Herd
B) Troop
C) Flock
D) Pack

Answers on Page # 87

Quiz # 10 - Groups of Animals

Q#4

What is a group of birds called when they are in flight together?

A) Flock
B) Gaggle
C) Colony
D) Swarm

Q#5

What is a group of geese called when they are on the ground together?

A) Flock
B) Gaggle
C) Herd
D) Troop

Q#6

What is a group of bees called?

A) Herd
B) Troop
C) Swarm
D) Colony

Q#7

What is a group of kangaroos called?

A) Flock
B) Herd
C) Pack
D) Mob

Answers on Page # 87

Quiz # 10 - Groups of Animals

Q#8
What is a group of ants called?

A) Troop
B) Herd
C) Army
D) Swarm

Q#9
What is a group of elephants called?

A) Troop
B) Herd
C) Pack
D) Mob

Q#10
What is a group of rhinoceroses called?

A) Crash
B) Herd
C) Colony
D) Flock

Q#11
What is a group of crows called?

A) Troop
B) Herd
C) Murder
D) Pod

Answers on Page # 87

Quiz # 10 - Groups of Animals

Q#12

What is a group of ravens called?

A) Unkindness
B) Herd
C) Pack
D) Flock

Q#13

What is a group of zebras called?

A) Troop
B) Dazzle
C) Pack
D) Flock

Q#14

What is a group of hawks called?

A) Troop
B) Swarm
C) Flight
D) Cast

Q#15

What is a group of penguins called?

A) Colony
B) Herd
C) Troop
D) Flock

Answers on Page # 87

Quiz # 11

Animals Anatomy

Q#1
Which part of a bird's body allows it to fly?

A) Gills
B) Beak
C) Fins
D) Wings

Q#2
What is the function of the udder in female mammals, including cows, goats, and sheep?

A) Respiration
B) Reproduction
C) Milk production
D) Digestion

Q#3
In snakes, what is the name of the heat-sensing organ located between the eye and the nostril?

A) Pit organ
B) Jacobson's organ
C) Ampulla
D) Gular sac

Answers on Page # 87

Quiz # 11 - Animals Anatomy

Q#4

What is the outermost layer of an insect's exoskeleton called?

A) Epidermis
B) Endodermis
C) Cuticle
D) Exodermis

Q#5

What is the pigment responsible for the color of animals skin and hair?

A) Hemoglobin
B) Melanin
C) Carotene
D) Bilirubin

Q#6

Which part of the animals eye controls the amount of light entering the pupil?

A) Lens
B) Cornea
C) Retina
D) Iris

Q#7

What is the hard outer covering of insects called?

A) Exoskeleton
B) Endoskeleton
C) Shell
D) Carapace

Answers on Page # 87

Quiz # 11 - Animals Anatomy

Q#8
Which part of a fish allows it to extract oxygen from water?

A) Skin
B) Fins
C) Lungs
D) Gills

Q#9
What is the specialized structure in a shark's nose that detects electrical signals from prey?

A) Ampulla of Lorenzini
B) Olfactory bulb
C) Jacobson's organ
D) Gular sac

Q#10
What is the name of the hard structure that makes up the outermost layer of a bird's beak?

A) Mandible
B) Maxilla
C) Rhamphotheca
D) Uvula

Q#11
Which part of a fish's body is responsible for maintaining buoyancy?

A) Fins
B) Swim bladder
C) Scales
D) Gills

Answers on Page # 87

Quiz # 11 - Animals Anatomy

Q#12

Which part of a mammal's ear is responsible for converting sound vibrations into electrical signals?

A) Cochlea
B) Tympanic membrane
C) Vestibule
D) Incus

Q#13

What is the term for the specialized hairs on a cat's face that assist in sensing its surroundings?

A) Quills
B) Fur
C) Mane
D) Whiskers

Q#14

What part of a bird's body produces their melodic songs?

A) Larynx
B) Beak
C) Tongue
D) Syrinx

Q#15

What is the primary function of a bird's beak?

A) Hearing
B) Smelling
C) Feeding
D) Breathing

Answers on Page # 87

Quiz # 12

Desert Dwellers

Q#1

Which desert dweller is known as the "ship of the desert" due to its ability to carry heavy loads over long distances?

A) Kangaroo Rat
B) Gila Monster
C) Camel
D) Elephant

Q#2

The largest hot desert in the world is in which country?

A) Australia
B) Sahara
C) Antarctica
D) Kuwait

Q#3

Which venomous snake is known for its rattling tail and is commonly found in North American deserts?

A) Gila Monster
B) Rattlesnake
C) Sidewinder
D) Cobra

Answers on Page # 87

Quiz # 12 - Desert Dwellers

Q#4
What is the name of the world's smallest fox, who lives in the African Desert region?

A) Micro Fox
B) Red Fox
C) Silver Fox
D) Fennec Fox

Q#5
Which nocturnal rodent is known for its ability to survive without drinking water, obtaining moisture from its food?

A) Jackrabbit
B) Kangaroo Rat
C) Scorpion
D) Lizard

Q#6
What is the primary diet of a desert scorpion?

A) Nectar
B) Small mammals
C) Other scorpions
D) Moonlight

Q#7
What is the name of the snake that makes an interesting S pattern in the sand when it moves?

A) Rattlesnake
B) Garter snake
C) Cobra
D) Sidewinder

Answers on Page # 87

Quiz # 12 - Desert Dwellers

Q#8
What is the primary function of the spines on a cactus in the desert?

A) To deter predators
B) To attract pollinators
C) To provide shade
D) To store water

Q#9
Which desert-dwelling insect is known for its loud chirping sound produced by rubbing its wings together?

A) Beetle
B) Shrimp
C) Spider
D) Cricket

Q#10
What spider catches its prey by running and attacking it?

A) Black Widow Spider
B) Wolf Spider
C) Brown Recluse Spider
D) Trap Door Spider

Q#11
Which of the following desert lizards can run on two legs?

A) Collard Lizard
B) Horned Liard
C) Iguanna
D) Leopard Lizard

Answers on Page # 87

Quiz # 12 - Desert Dwellers

Q#12

Which venomous desert dweller is known for its painful sting?

A) Gila Monster
B) Desert iguana
C) Scorpion
D) Spider

Q#13

What fast-running bird is so quick it can catch rattlesnakes?

A) Ostrich
B) Roadrunner
C) Sparrow
D) Falcon

Q#14

What is the main adaptation of the dromedary camel for desert life?

A) Ability to hibernate
B) Extra-long legs
C) Water storage in hump
D) Ability to fly

Q#15

Where do sand cats typically live?

A) Mountains
B) Burrows in the ground
C) Trees
D) Underwater

Answers on Page # 87

Quiz # 13

Animals Feeding Styles

Q#1

What type of animal primarily eats meat?

A) Carnivore
B) Herbivore
C) Omnivore
D) Insectivore

Q#2

What type of animal primarily eats plants?

A) Scavenger
B) Herbivore
C) Omnivore
D) Insectivore

Q#3

What is the term for an animal that eats both plants and animals?

A) Omnivore
B) Predator
C) Prey
D) Scavenger

Answers on Page # 88

Quiz # 13 - Animals Feeding Styles

Q#4
Which of these animals primarily feeds on grasses and leaves?

A) Wolf
B) Eagle
C) Cow
D) Crocodile

Q#5
Which of the following animals is a classic example of a carnivore?

A) Koala
B) Gorilla
C) Panda
D) Tiger

Q#6
What is the main food source for a panda?

A) Bamboo
B) Fish
C) Ants
D) Grasshoppers

Q#7
What type of teeth do herbivores typically have for grinding plant material?

A) Pointed premolars
B) Sharp incisors
C) Long canines
D) Flat molars

Answers on Page # 88

Quiz # 13 - Animals Feeding Styles

Q#8
Which of these animals primarily eats fruits, leaves, and shoots?

A) Vulture
B) Monkey
C) Fox
D) Alligator

Q#9
What type of diet is common for animals like hawks and eagles?

A) Piscivore
B) Herbivore
C) Omnivore
D) Carnivore

Q#10
Which organ is more complex in herbivores compared to carnivores?

A) Saliva
B) Enzymes
C) Stomach
D) Liver

Q#11
What is the primary diet of a herbivorous animal like a giraffe?

A) Small mammals
B) Fish
C) Insects
D) Leaves

Answers on Page # 88

Quiz # 13 - Animals Feeding Styles

Q#12

What type of animal primarily consumes insects and small invertebrates?

A) Insectivore
B) Herbivore
C) Carnivore
D) Omnivore

Q#13

What type of diet does a rabbit follow?

A) Omnivore
B) Carnivore
C) Herbivore
D) Piscivore

Q#14

Which of these animals primarily eats grass and plants?

A) Hyena
B) Eagle
C) Fox
D) Horse

Q#15

Which animal primarily eats other animals and is known for its hunting prowess?

A) Leopard
B) Giraffe
C) Hippopotamus
D) Rhinoceros

Answers on Page # 88

Quiz # 14

Deadliest Animals

Q#1

Which animal causes the highest number of human fatalities each year?

A) Mosquitoes

B) Snakes

C) Lions

D) Crocodiles

Q#2

According to scientists, an attack on a person by which of these animals is most likely to kill the person?

A) Elephant

B) Lion

C) Black Mamba

D) Hippo

Q#3

The stings of which creature kills hundreds of swimmers each year?

A) Scorpionfish

B) Jellyfish

C) Electric Eel

D) Cone Snail

Answers on Page # 88

Quiz # 14 - Deadliest Animals

Q#4

Which animal is the primary transmitter of the Rabies in world?

A) Rabbits
B) Monkeys
C) Dogs
D) Ticks

Q#5

Which of these animals has the strongest recorded jaw strength?

A) Saltwater Crocodile
B) Hippopotamus
C) Lion
D) Bear

Q#6

Which shark is often considered more dangerous to people than the great white, because it can swim in fresh water?

A) Nurse Shark
B) Hammerhead Shark
C) Tiger Shark
D) Bull Shark

Q#7

The bite of which animal is roughly equivalent to a bee sting?

A) Mosquitoe
B) Tarantula
C) Scorpion
D) Ant

Answers on Page # 88

Quiz # 14 - Deadliest Animals

Q#8
Which of these African animals is nicknamed "Black Death"?

A) African Elephant
B) Black Mamba
C) Cape Buffalo
D) Hippopotamus

Q#9
What is the deadliest big cat in terms of human attacks?

A) African Lion
B) Bengal Tiger
C) Leopard
D) Cougar

Q#10
What is the most venomous fish in the world, known for its venomous dorsal spines?

A) Stonefish
B) Lionfish
C) Pufferfish
D) Clownfish

Q#11
Which tiny arachnid is responsible for spreading Lyme disease through its bite?

A) Spiders
B) Mites
C) Scorpions
D) Ticks

Answers on Page # 88

Quiz # 14 - Deadliest Animals

Q#12
Which fish, known for its sharp teeth and aggressive behavior, is found in the waters of the Amazon Basin?

A) Discus Fish
B) Angelfish
C) Piranha
D) Oscar Fish

Q#13
Which snake species is responsible for the most snakebite deaths in Africa?

A) Boomslang
B) Black Mamba
C) Gaboon Viper
D) Puff Adder

Q#14
What is the world's largest venomous lizard?

A) Komodo Dragon
B) Gila Monster
C) Bearded Dragon
D) Nile Monitor

Q#15
Which animal's sting is often called "the world's most painful"?

A) Tarantula Hawk
B) Honey Bee
C) Bullet Ant
D) Paper Wasp

Answers on Page # 88

Quiz # 15

All about Dogs

Q#1

What is the term for a male dog?

A) Bitch
B) Pup
C) Sire
D) Stud

Q#2

Which dog breed is known for its wrinkled skin and loose jowls?

A) Labrador Retriever
B) Bulldog
C) Dalmatian
D) Greyhound

Q#3

What is the smallest recognized dog breed?

A) Chihuahua
B) Golden Retriever
C) Siberian Husky
D) Beagle

Answers on Page # 88

Quiz # 15 - All about Dogs

Q#4
How many teeth does an adult dog have?

A) 28
B) 36
C) 42
D) 44

Q#5
Which breed is known for its distinctive blue-black tongue?

A) Shih Tzu
B) Rottweiler
C) Pomeranian
D) Chow Chow

Q#6
What is the term for a group of puppies born to the same mother at the same time?

A) Litter
B) Flock
C) Pod
D) Pack

Q#7
Which breed is often referred to as the "King of Terriers"?

A) Bull Terrier
B) Boston Terrier
C) Yorkshire Terrier
D) Airedale Terrier

Answers on Page # 88

Quiz # 15 - All about Dogs

Q#8
What is the average lifespan of a medium-sized dog?

A) 5-8 years
B) 10-13 years
C) 15-18 years
D) 20-25 years

Q#9
Which breed is known for its distinctive spotted coat?

A) Dachshund
B) Basset Hound
C) Boxer
D) Dalmatian

Q#10
What is the term for a dog's sense of smell that allows it to detect scents over long distances?

A) Vision
B) Taste
C) Olfaction
D) Hearing

Q#11
What is the term for a dog's ability to communicate and understand human emotions, such as joy or sadness?

A) Empathy
B) Sympathy
C) Telepathy
D) Aggression

Answers on Page # 88

Quiz # 15 - All about Dogs

Q#12
Which breed is often considered one of the fastest-running dog breeds and is used in greyhound racing?

A) Dachshund
B) Labrador Retriever
C) Boxer
D) Greyhound

Q#13
Which breed of dog is considered the smartest?

A) German Shepherd
B) Border Collie
C) Fox Terrier
D) Spaniel

Q#14
What type of dog does the queen of England used to have?

A) Bullterrier
B) King Charles Spaniel
C) Fox Terrier
D) Corgi

Q#15
Why do dogs lick their owners?

A) To clean them
B) To show affection
C) To taste their skin
D) To mark them with scent

Answers on Page # 88

Quiz # 16

All about Cats

Q#1

Which breed is known for its hairless appearance?

A) Sphynx
B) Siamese
C) Persian
D) Maine Coon

Q#2

What is the normal body temperature of a healthy cat in degrees Fahrenheit (approximate)?

A) 85°F
B) 94°F
C) 101.5°F
D) 110°F

Q#3

What is the largest domesticated cat breed?

A) Bengal
B) Siamese
C) Ragdoll
D) Maine Coon

Answers on Page # 88

Quiz # 16 - All about Cats

Q#4
What is the average lifespan of a pet cat?

A) 5-8 years
B) 10-13 years
C) 15-18 years
D) 20-25 years

Q#5
What breed of cat has no tail?

A) Sphynx
B) Exotic Longhair
C) British Shorthair
D) Manx

Q#6
Which breed is famous for its "folded" ears that bend forward and downward?

A) Burmese
B) Scottish Fold
C) Abyssinian
D) Persian

Q#7
How fast can a house cat run?

A) 20 mph
B) 25 mph
C) 30 mph
D) 35 mph

Answers on Page # 88

Q#8
What is the average number of hours a cat sleeps per day?

A) 4-6 hours
B) 8-10 hours
C) 12-16 hours
D) 18-20 hours

Q#9
How many whiskers does the average cat have?

A) 10
B) 14
C) 24
D) 34

Q#10
What is the term for a cat's ability to land safely on its feet after a fall?

A) Grace
B) Agility
C) Flexibility
D) Righting reflex

Q#11
What breed of cat has a reputation for being cross-eyed?

A) Savanah
B) American Shorthair
C) Siamese
D) Ragdoll

Answers on Page # 88

Quiz # 16 - All about Cats

Q#12

In which major tourist attraction are hundreds of cats used for mice control?

A) Disneyland
B) Tower of Landon
C) The White House
D) Statue of Liberty

Q#13

Who was the first US president to have a cat in the White House?

A) Theodore Roosevelt
B) Abraham Lincoln
C) Bill Clinton
D) John F Kennedy

Q#14

Through which part of their bodies do cats sweat?

A) Paws
B) Tongue
C) Fur
D) Skin

Q#15

How far can a cat rotate its ears?

A) 100 degrees
B) 270 degrees
C) 180 degrees
D) 90 degrees

Answers on Page # 88

Quiz # 17

Endangered Species

Q#1
Which large cat species is critically endangered due to habitat loss and poaching?

A) Amur leopards
B) Cheetah
C) Snow Leopard
D) African Lion

Q#2
What is the world's smallest marine mammal, often threatened by fishing nets and habitat degradation?

A) Sea Otter
B) Manatee
C) Vaquita
D) Dolphin

Q#3
Which species of great ape, closely related to humans, is critically endangered?

A) Bonobo
B) Gorilla
C) Chimpanzee
D) Orangutan

Answers on Page # 88

Quiz # 17 - Endangered Species

Q#4
What is the largest species of sea turtle, facing threats from fishing gear, pollution, and habitat loss?

A) Loggerhead Turtle
B) Leatherback Turtle
C) Green Turtle
D) Hawksbill Turtle

Q#5
Which big cat, native to South America, is critically endangered ?

A) Jaguar
B) Cougar
C) Ocelot
D) Puma

Q#6
What is the name of the critically endangered rhinoceros with two horns found in Southeast Asia?

A) White Rhinoceros
B) Indian Rhinoceros
C) Woolly Rhinoceros
D) Sumatran Rhinoceros

Q#7
What is the largest vulture species, facing a declining population?

A) Turkey Vulture
B) Griffon Vulture
C) White-rumped vulture
D) Rüppell's Vulture

Answers on Page # 88

Quiz # 17 - Endangered Species

Q#8
What is the critically endangered species of marine turtle that nests on the beaches of the Arabian Peninsula?

A) Loggerhead Turtle
B) Leatherback Turtle
C) Olive Ridley Turtle
D) Hawksbill Turtle

Q#9
Which marine animal, often called a "living fossil," is critically endangered due to bycatch and habitat loss?

A) Coelacanth
B) Giant Squid
C) Chambered Nautilus
D) Mantis Shrimp

Q#10
Which species of pangolin is critically endangered, primarily due to illegal trade for their scales?

A) Palawan Pangolin
B) Indian Pangolin
C) Sunda Pangolin
D) Giant Pangolin

Q#11
Which species of great ape is critically endangered, primarily due to habitat destruction and poaching for the pet trade?

A) Orangutan
B) Gorilla
C) Chimpanzee
D) Bonobo

Answers on Page # 88

Quiz # 17 - Endangered Species

Q#12
Which species of penguin, listed as endangered due to habitat loss and oil spills?

A) African Penguin
B) King Penguin
C) Little Blue Penguin
D) Galápagos Penguin

Q#13
Which species of sea otter is critically endangered due to habitat loss and oil spills?

A) European Otter
B) Northern Sea Otter
C) Southern Sea Otter
D) Giant Otter

Q#14
What is the world's smallest bear species, listed as endangered?

A) Polar Bear
B) Sun Bear
C) Giant Panda
D) Sloth Bear

Q#15
Which bird, native to New Zealand, is critically endangered due to habitat loss and invasive predators?

A) Kakapo Parrot
B) Kea Parrot
C) Takahe
D) Kiwi

Answers on Page # 88

Quiz # 18

Prehistoric Creatures

Q#1

Which group of prehistoric reptiles included species like Tyrannosaurus rex and Velociraptor?

A) Pterosaurs
B) Sauropods
C) Theropods
D) Ornithopods

Q#2

What is the name of the largest-known flying reptile from the time of the dinosaurs, with a wingspan of up to 40 feet?

A) Pteranodon
B) Quetzalcoatlus
C) Dimorphodon
D) Rhamphorhynchus

Q#3

Which prehistoric mammal, often mistaken for a dinosaur, lived during the Ice Age and had long, curved tusks?

A) Woolly Mammoth
B) Saber-Toothed Tiger
C) Glyptodon
D) Megalodon

Answers on Page # 88

Quiz # 18 - Prehistoric Creatures

Q#4

What is the term for the flying reptiles that lived during the time of the dinosaurs and were not dinosaurs themselves?

A) Plesiosaurs
B) Spinosaurus
C) Ichthyosaurs
D) Pterosaurs

Q#5

What is the largest known prehistoric shark species, often called the "megashark"?

A) Megalodon
B) Dunkleosteus
C) Liopleurodon
D) Mosasaurus

Q#6

What is the name of the large, herbivorous dinosaur with a distinctive bony frill and three facial horns on its head?

A) Brachiosaurus
B) Triceratops
C) Stegosaurus
D) Ankylosaurus

Q#7

What is the most famous and well-preserved woolly mammoth specimen found in Siberia?

A) Dima
B) Lyuba
C) Yuka
D) Buttercup

Answers on Page # 88

Quiz # 18 - Prehistoric Creatures

Q#8
Which prehistoric birds similar to modern birds lived with dinosaurs?

A) Pterosaurs
B) Plesiosaurs
C) Ichthyosaurs
D) Archaeopteryx

Q#9
What was the name of the prehistoric sea scorpion during the Carboniferous period?

A) Trilobite
B) Eurypterid
C) Ammonite
D) Anomalocaris

Q#10
Which prehistoric reptile is famous for its sail-like dorsal fin and lived during the Permian period?

A) Dimetrodon
B) Anomalocaris
C) Ichthyosaurus
D) Tylosaurus

Q#11
Which prehistoric mammal was one of the largest marsupials and lived in Australia during the Pleistocene epoch?

A) Zygomaturus
B) Thylacoleo
C) Diprotodon
D) Palorchestes

Answers on Page # 88

Quiz # 18 - Prehistoric Creatures

Q#12

Which prehistoric reptile was a marine predator with a crocodile-like body and lived during the Cretaceous period?

A) Kronosaurus
B) Tylosaurus
C) Liopleurodon
D) Mosasaurus

Q#13

What is the largest known prehistoric snake, with an estimated length of up to 42 feet?

A) Gastornis
B) Hesperornis
C) Moa
D) Phorusrhacos

Q#14

What is the largest known prehistoric spider, with a leg span of up to 12 inches?

A) Megarachne
B) Arthropleura
C) Pulmonoscorpius
D) Mesothelae

Q#15

What is the largest known prehistoric turtle, with a shell length of up to 13 feet?

A) Peloneustes
B) Stupendemys
C) Proganochelys
D) Archelon

Answers on Page # 88

Quiz # 19

Animals Senses

Q#1

What is the primary sense used by bats to navigate and locate prey in the dark?

A) Smell
B) Touch
C) Echolocation
D) Taste

Q#2

Which sense is most highly developed in dogs, allowing them to detect scents over great distances?

A) Sight
B) Hearing
C) Taste
D) Smell

Q#3

Which animal is known for its extraordinary night vision?

A) Owl
B) Kangaroo
C) Sloth
D) Armadillo

Answers on Page # 89

Quiz # 19 - Animals Senses

Q#4

Which animal is known for its ability to sense electrical fields in the water to locate prey?

A) Octopus
B) Shark
C) Seahorse
D) Clownfish

Q#5

What is the term for the sense that allows birds to detect the Earth's magnetic field for navigation during migration?

A) Electrosense
B) Thermosense
C) Magnetosense
D) Hydrosense

Q#6

Which sense is highly developed in cats, enabling them to see well in low light conditions?

A) Hearing
B) Taste
C) Smell
D) Night Vision

Q#7

Which animal has the ability to taste through its feet?

A) Butterfly
B) Spider
C) Lizard
D) Ant

Answers on Page # 89

Quiz # 19 - Animals Senses

Q#8

Which sense is used by certain fish to detect changes in water pressure, helping them navigate at different depths?

A) Electrosense
B) Magnetosense
C) Thermosense
D) Barosense

Q#9

What is the primary sense used by dolphins and whales for communication and navigation underwater?

A) Sight
B) Taste
C) Echolocation
D) Smell

Q#10

What is the sense that allows certain birds, like vultures, to locate carrion from great distances using smell?

A) Magnetosense
B) Thermosense
C) Electrosense
D) Olfactory Sense

Q#11

What is the primary sense used by a homing pigeon to find its way back to its home loft over long distances?

A) Magnetoreception
B) Smell
C) Sight
D) Hearing

Answers on Page # 89

Quiz # 19 - Animals Senses

Q#12

What is the name of the sense that allows certain fish to detect changes in water temperature?

A) Electrosense
B) Thermosense
C) Magnetosense
D) Hydrosense

Q#13

Which sense is highly developed in eagles and hawks, enabling them to spot prey from great heights?

A) Hearing
B) Smell
C) Sight
D) Taste

Q#14

Which animal is known for its ability to detect changes in the Earth's magnetic field and use it for navigation?

A) Sea Turtle
B) Lemur
C) Sea Lion
D) Salmon

Q#15

Which sense is crucial for some species of ants to communicate with one another through the release of chemical signals?

A) Taste
B) Touch
C) Smell
D) Pheromone Sense

Answers on Page # 89

Quiz # 20

Animals Behavior & Communication

Q#1

What term describes an animal's seasonal movement to find food or breeding grounds?

A) Hibernation
B) Migration
C) Camouflage
D) Territorial

Q#2

Which social insects construct elaborate nests made of paper, often hanging from trees or structures?

A) Ants
B) Bees
C) Wasps
D) Termites

Q#3

How do honeybees communicate the location of a food source to their hive mates?

A) Dance
B) Sing
C) Blink
D) Whistle

Answers on Page # 89

Quiz # 20 - Animals Behavior & Communication

Q#4

Which animal is known for its ability to use tools, including sticks to extract termites from mounds?

A) Chimpanzee
B) Giraffe
C) Koala
D) Kangaroo

Q#5

Which bird is famous for its ability to mimic a wide range of sounds, including human speech?

A) Raven
B) Bald Eagle
C) Parrot
D) Pigeon

Q#6

Which marine mammal is known for its complex songs that can last for hours and travel long distances underwater?

A) Dolphin
B) Whale
C) Seal
D) Manatee

Q#7

What is the process of animals shedding old feathers, skin, or shells to allow new growth?

A) Hibernation
B) Camouflage
C) Territorial
D) Moulting

Answers on Page # 89

Q#8
Which type of communication involves chemical signals, such as pheromones, to convey information to other animals?

A) Vocalization
B) Olfactory
C) Visual
D) Tactile

Q#9
What term describes an animal's ability to blend into its surroundings to avoid detection by predators or prey?

A) Hibernation
B) Migration
C) Camouflage
D) Territorial

Q#10
How do ants communicate with each other by leaving a trail for others to follow to a food source?

A) Sound signals
B) Visual signals
C) Tactile signals
D) Chemical signals

Q#11
How do male crickets attract females for mating?

A) Singing
B) Dancing
C) Flashing
D) Fighting

Answers on Page # 89

Quiz # 20 - Animals Behavior & Communication

Q#12
What is the term for a group of wolves working together to hunt for food?

A) Pack
B) Herd
C) Flock
D) Swarm

Q#13
Which animal is famous for its courtship dance, which includes intricate footwork and colorful displays?

A) Sloth
B) Peacock
C) Hedgehog
D) Armadillo

Q#14
What is the process by which some animals enter a dormant state during harsh environmental conditions, such as winter?

A) Hibernation
B) Molting
C) Camouflage
D) Territorial

Q#15
Which insect is known for its complex dances that convey the location of food sources to other members of the colony?

A) Ants
B) Bees
C) Wasps
D) Termites

Answers on Page # 89

Answers

Answers

Quiz # 1
1. Bat
2. Kangaroo
3. Cheetah
4. Lion
5. Polar Bear
6. Sloth
7. Bison
8. Giant Panda
9. Blue Whale
10. Grizzly Bear
11. Axolotl
12. Zebra
13. Platypus
14. Elephant
15. Armadillo

Quiz # 2
1. Jaguar
2. Elephant
3. Sun Bear
4. Ibex
5. Spider Monkey
6. Lemur
7. Eland
8. Kangaroo
9. Alligator
10. Bald Eagle
11. Alpha
12. White Rhinoceros
13. Ostrich
14. Bengal Tiger
15. Lion

Quiz # 3
1. Toucan
2. Osprey
3. Bee Hummingbird
4. Falcon
5. Flippers
6. Pelican
7. Kiwi
8. Peregrine Falcon
9. Eagle Owl
10. Peahen
11. Parliament
12. Plankton
13. Dove
14. Gray Jay
15. Victoria crowned pigeon

Quiz # 4
1. Whale Shark
2. Pod
3. Narwhal
4. Manta Ray
5. Plankton
6. Cuttlefish
7. Dwarf Sperm Whale
8. Starfish
9. Jellyfish
10. Firefly Squid
11. Photosynthesis
12. Seamounts
13. Sea Anemone
14. Manatee
15. Giant Squid

Quiz # 5
1. Puppy
2. Kitten
3. Foal
4. Cub
5. Fawn
6. Calf
7. Joey
8. Kid
9. Piglet
10. Kit
11. Duckling
12. Pup
13. Calf
14. Tadpole
15. Hatchling

Quiz # 6
1. Dog
2. Parrot
3. Goldfish
4. Sheep
5. Dogs
6. 10-15 years
7. Felis catus
8. Clowder
9. Tom
10. Holland Lop
11. Shar-Pei
12. Mare
13. Manx
14. Hamster
15. Chameleon

Answers

Quiz # 7
1. United States
2. Springbok
3. Brown Bear
4. Markhor
5. China
6. Elephant
7. Rufous Hornero
8. Dolphin
9. Jaguar
10. Lion
11. Kiwi
12. Elk
13. Peacock
14. Cow
15. Beaver

Quiz # 8
1. Anaconda
2. Leatherback Turtle
3. Goliath Frog
4. Scales
5. Chameleon
6. Saltwater Crocodile
7. Rattlesnake
8. Pit Organs
9. Cobra
10. Tuatara
11. Autotomy
12. Toe Pads
13. Basilisk Lizard
14. Frog
15. Spectacle

Quiz # 9
1. Cheetah
2. King Cobra
3. Leatherback Sea Turtle
4. Falabella
5. Chameleon
6. Red Kangaroo
7. Hector's Dolphin
8. Shire Horse
9. Elf Owl
10. Koala
11. Lyrebird
12. Hummingbird
13. Capybara
14. Fennec Fox
15. Snail

Quiz # 10
1. Pride
2. School
3. Pack
4. Flock
5. Gaggle
6. Swarm
7. Mob
8. Army
9. Herd
10. Crash
11. Murder
12. Unkindness
13. Dazzle
14. Cast
15. Colony

Quiz # 11
1. Wings
2. Milk production
3. Pit organ
4. Cuticle
5. Melanin
6. Iris
7. Exoskeleton
8. Gills
9. Ampulla of Lorenzini
10. Rhamphotheca
11. Swim bladder
12. Cochlea
13. Whiskers
14. Syrinx
15. Feeding

Quiz # 12
1. Camel
2. Australia
3. Rattlesnake
4. Fennec Fox
5. Kangaroo Rat
6. Other scorpions
7. Sidewinder
8. To deter predators
9. Cricket
10. Wolf Spider
11. Collard Lizard
12. Scorpion
13. Roadrunner
14. Water storage in hump
15. Burrows in the ground

Answers

Quiz # 13

1. Carnivore
2. Herbivore
3. Omnivore
4. Cow
5. Tiger
6. Bamboo
7. Flat molars
8. Monkey
9. Carnivore
10. Stomach
11. Leaves
12. Insectivore
13. Herbivore
14. Horse
15. Leopard

Quiz # 14

1. Mosquitoes
2. Hippo
3. Jellyfish
4. Dogs
5. Saltwater Crocodile
6. Bull Shark
7. Tarantula
8. Cape Buffalo
9. Bengal Tiger
10. Stonefish
11. Ticks
12. Piranha
13. Puff Adder
14. Komodo Dragon
15. Bullet Ant

Quiz # 15

1. Stud
2. Bulldog
3. Chihuahua
4. 42
5. Chow Chow
6. Litter
7. Airedale Terrier
8. 10-13 years
9. Dalmatian
10. Olfaction
11. Empathy
12. Greyhound
13. Border Collie
14. Corgi
15. To show affection

Quiz # 16

1. Sphynx
2. 101.5°F
3. Maine Coon
4. 15-18 years
5. Manx
6. Scottish Fold
7. 30 mph
8. 12-16 hours
9. 24
10. Righting reflex
11. Siamese
12. Disneyland
13. Abraham Lincoln
14. Paws
15. 180 degrees

Quiz # 17

1. Amur leopards
2. Vaquita
3. Orangutan
4. Leatherback Turtle
5. Jaguar
6. Sumatran Rhinoceros
7. White-rumped vulture
8. Hawksbill Turtle
9. Coelacanth
10. Sunda Pangolin
11. Bonobo
12. African Penguin
13. Southern Sea Otter
14. Sun Bear
15. Kakapo Parrot

Quiz # 18

1. Theropods
2. Quetzalcoatlus
3. Woolly Mammoth
4. Pterosaurs
5. Megalodon
6. Triceratops
7. Yuka
8. Archaeopteryx
9. Eurypterid
10. Dimetrodon
11. Diprotodon
12. Mosasaurus
13. Moa
14. Megarachne
15. Archelon

Answers

Quiz # 19

1. Echolocation
2. Smell
3. Owl
4. Shark
5. Magnetosense
6. Night Vision
7. Butterfly
8. Barosense
9. Echolocation
10. Olfactory Sense
11. Magnetoreception
12. Thermosense
13. Sight
14. Sea Turtle
15. Pheromone Sense

Quiz # 20

1. Migration
2. Wasps
3. Dance
4. Chimpanzee
5. Parrot
6. Whale
7. Moulting
8. Olfactory
9. Camouflage
10. Chemical signals
11. Singing
12. Pack
13. Peacock
14. Hibernation
15. Bees

SHARP MINDS
Learning

Thank you for choosing and trusting us!

Don't forget to share your experience and give a review.

sharpmindslearning.com

www.ingramcontent.com/pod-product-compliance
Lightning Source LLC
Chambersburg PA
CBHW042119100526
44587CB00025B/4116